Historical, Hysterical Tangents

Target Audience: Middle School Readers, Ages: 9-13
Genre: Narrative, Creative Nonfiction
Author: Wendy D. Ward
Illustrator: Jack Martinez
Copyright © 2025 by PUN UNINTENDED PUBLISHING ™
ISBN: 979-8-218-77352-6

To the world, I leave my knowledge.

To my children, I leave my **legacy**.

Keep a light on.

Historical, Hysterical Tangents – Book 1

This first book launches a *learning-focused* series created to enrich community, celebrate culture, and elevate the craft of writing—an independent literary movement dedicated to nurturing **creative nonfiction**, one true story at a time.

Although you will laugh, maybe cry (from laughing, of course) while reading this collection of crazy tangents, you'll also learn real history, a little science, new words to expand your vocabulary, and most importantly, **you will discover puns**. Not sure what a pun is? You will find out once you get to the meat and potatoes (the actual content), so get ready to dig in! — Sound exciting? … Well, I'd say so if you want to become even **smarter**, more **popular**, and in the future, earn more money by using your **education** to open doors! I mean, unless you dislike money, don't value opportunities only offered through education, or you're in **love** with the idea of having the door slammed in your face. **Ouch**.

Curated as a **critical thinking** component, this resource was intended for classroom learning, just as much as it was meant for recreational **fun**.

Support. Share. Succeed.

AKNOWLEDGEMENTS

Those who inspire me most deserve an overwhelming amount of gratitude, starting with my kids, **Hannah** and **Hunter**. Both outgrew me in middle school; they also stand behind me with confidence while I pursue remarkable things. Filling my life with love and purpose, they are the reasons I'm committed to living my best life.

As an educator, I also find inspiration in the classroom. It's a perk that comes with the job. My students drive me to deliver more; yet there are too many to name individually. Without their support, I'd be up a stream in a pontoon boat with a broken motor. Gaining momentum from their enthusiasm toward my work, I was able to simply start. I began my research and writing, and that is where it all came together.

Starting out, my strategy was undeveloped, and my vision was cloudy, but once I got going, I was operating like a steamboat headed downstream. I owe a special thanks to a giant motivating force, Jack Martinez, a unique artist, well recognized as a scholar, animator, and collaborator. After discovering his drawing talent in class, he and I partnered together on this project. Coming from a background in animation, he dove deep into a new world of illustration for print and floated right to the top.

Grounding myself in my work comes easy. While immersing myself in research, writing, and designing the precise layout of each page as I develop my next story, I can easily lose track of where I belong in the real world; therefore, my appreciation flows like warm molasses to Amber Rose Godden; as a supporter, confidante, editor, and main contributor toward my success, she aims to keep my compass needle sharp, so I don't miss a turn on the map.

Giving ode to my mother, grandmother, aunts, cousins, and entire family, those who have loved me and believed in me since the beginning of time is vital; without them, I'm no one and my accomplishments are meaningless.

Above all, I thank **God** for my blessings. Showing recognition is paramount.

CONTENTS

- ◇ **About the Book**
- ◇ **Acknowledgements**
- ◇ **Contents**

- ◇ **Glossary**
- ◇ **Bibliography**
- ◇ **Index**
- ◇ **About the Author**
- ◇ **About the Illustrator**

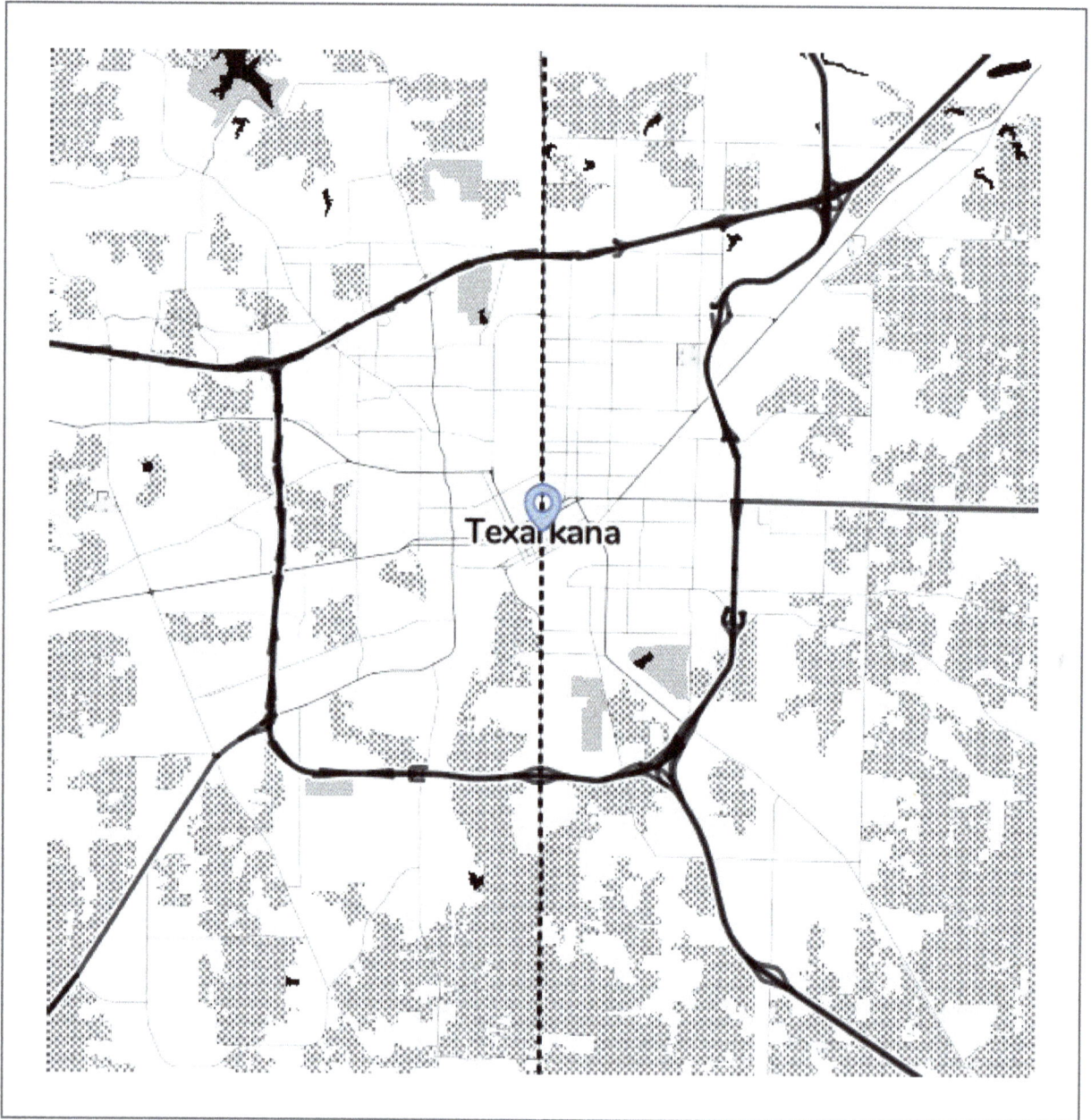

A map of Texarkana.

CHAPTER 1

Starting with a blip about history...

A True, Unreelistic Story About the Day it Rained Fish in Texarkana

BOOM! It all started with a loud crack of thunder!

(Wendy, the school's historian, began over the loudspeaker...)

Texarkana, a quaint little town that lies on the Texas-Arkansas state line, was under the threat of severe weather. More accurately, the threat of unusual weather.

Very unusual.

On this day, December 29, 2021, Gary Chatelian, a meteorologist from the National Weather Service advised, it is truly odd for fish to descend from the sky, but claims, it can happen!

Wait. What? Fish? Raining Fish, you ask?

Yes. It is true.

"Fish can be picked up in a water spot or tornadic winds," he said.

Further explaining, he went on to say, "They are picked up with the wind and come down like any debris does. They could have been picked up somewhere like Lake Texoma; they could have come from anywhere; and whatever goes up, must come down."

Duh, I thought to myself when I read his statement in the newspaper, not his whole statement, just the end part. The law of gravity.

Isn't that common knowledge?

I rolled my eyes, but honestly, it's the only part that makes sense.

Okay, there's more to this fishy story, but I truly still have a tough time imagining these outrageous weather conditions, and now that I'm aware, I am paranoid. Uneasy. Worried. Concerned. I am afraid that the day will come when I have a similar firsthand experience. Will I be prepared? How does one prepare for the unexpected? I mean if you don't know what to expect. Now, just knowing poses a new life challenge; this is something I never had to worry about in the past.

Part of me wants to unread the news article, part of me wants to know more! Knowledge is power, so I'll go on.

Although this phenomenon has never been observed by scientists, a local reporter in Texarkana noted that he personally witnessed a dozen, maybe two dozen, shiny silver fish lying on the ground; they were described as two to six inches in length, resembling shad, or small bass.

There were more eyewitnesses. Something in the air smelled fishy and the media jumped on it!

In this case, it was fish. Literally.

Take a moment. In your mind, conjure the smell of a fresh fish market, or the stench of a sushi restaurant. Consider the aquatic aroma in the air at the gulf seashore or the pungent marine scent you'd expect to breathe while spending a day at a sandy beach with your crazy uncle who caught zero fish due to his obnoxious behavior and lack of skills. Perhaps it was his strong cologne, a cheap bottle he got in his stocking last year; or was it his body odor the cologne was masking?

Maybe, his bad breath. Hard to tell.

Okay, I should get back to the story...

As you can imagine, anyone who saw the atrocity was confused, to say the least. Bystanders, reporters, and journalists were reeled in by the news!

In town, Discount Wheel & Tire and Tiger Stadium, both on Summerhill Road on the Texas side, called in to share their unreelistic experiences with the authorities.

The phone was ringing off the hook! Pun intended.

(*Wendy giggled aloud, as she pushed her glasses in place and went on...*)

The manager of Discount Wheel & Tire, Tim Brigham, told the Texarkana Gazette, "it started hailing and looked like there was about to be a tornado. Next thing I knew, there were fish falling." In fact, "they were bouncing off the concrete," he told Gazette reporter Lori Dunn.

Sadly, they all had busted heads.

Ouch.

So strange, right?! Almost unbelievable, so you may be thinking to yourself, someone make sense of this for me, please!

History will tell, raining creatures can occur from time to time, so this incident in Texarkana is not by any means a first.

Classified as 'animal rain,' reports of raining fish and frogs can be traced back as far back as the Roman Empire.

Oddly, raining bats, birds, jellyfish, and even—snakes can happen!

On the other hand, history does not tell us the kind of outerwear we should equip ourselves with in order to sustain this type of weather. Think about it! For a snowstorm, we wear heavy coats, hats, and gloves, along with a good pair of boots. On a hot sunny day, we wear sunscreen and loose, cool, lightweight, light-colored clothes to repel the sun as much as possible.

Imagine waking up, turning on the TV, and you hear the weather forecast: 'cloudy, high winds, with a 30% chance of animal rain.'

Yikes!

Do you dare go out? If so, what would you wear?

An armored suit? Multiple layers of clothing? Carry a fish net along with an extra durable umbrella, perhaps?

Stop for a moment. Contemplate. What would you do?

Are you prepared?

Seriously. Visualize yourself running to the school bus stop with the threat of severe, I mean, unusual weather of this nature?

Sounds like we should be prepared for anything. And Everything.

Just in case. Just saying.

Let me continue...

At sunset, when the storm cleared, Mr. Brigham at the tire shop had one of his employees pick up the fish that fell in front of his building and pile them around back to prevent customers from slipping on them in the parking lot.

Hilarious? Yes. A lawsuit for a business owner? I do not know. Dangerous? For sure! Stinky? No, not if you love the smell of raw fish as much as a stray cat.

Yes, uncooked.

Eewww...

I know, but I'm not judging. I mean if that's you. I promise, I'm not.

Honestly, who am I to judge? No one. Really. I love fish. A lot. More than my classmates, I'm sure. More than my family. I'm positive. Okay, maybe not the smell.

(*Wendy cracked a grin, knowing she's on the verge of another tangent. She reminded herself to stick to the story and went on to wrap it up before the first bell...*)

Down the street, at Tiger Stadium, the Texas High School boys' soccer team was released early from practice due to the weather.

The flounder-like aroma continued to permeate the steamy, humid air, while one player "kicked up" a slippery little silver fish from the sidelines as he walked off the wet field. What a day in Texarkana!

"...and that's all for today's historical, hysterical news," Wendy said, as she released the microphone button on the school's overhead PA system in the front office.

THE END

She headed back to class with a smile on her face. She genuinely loves History and enjoys sharing her knowledge with her peers.

The principal, listening from her desk, was still taking it all in.

Envision a deer in the headlights.

"Very interesting! Where does she find these stories!?" ... she wondered aloud, laughing all the way to the teacher's lounge for another cup of coffee. French roast. No sugar. A ton of cream.

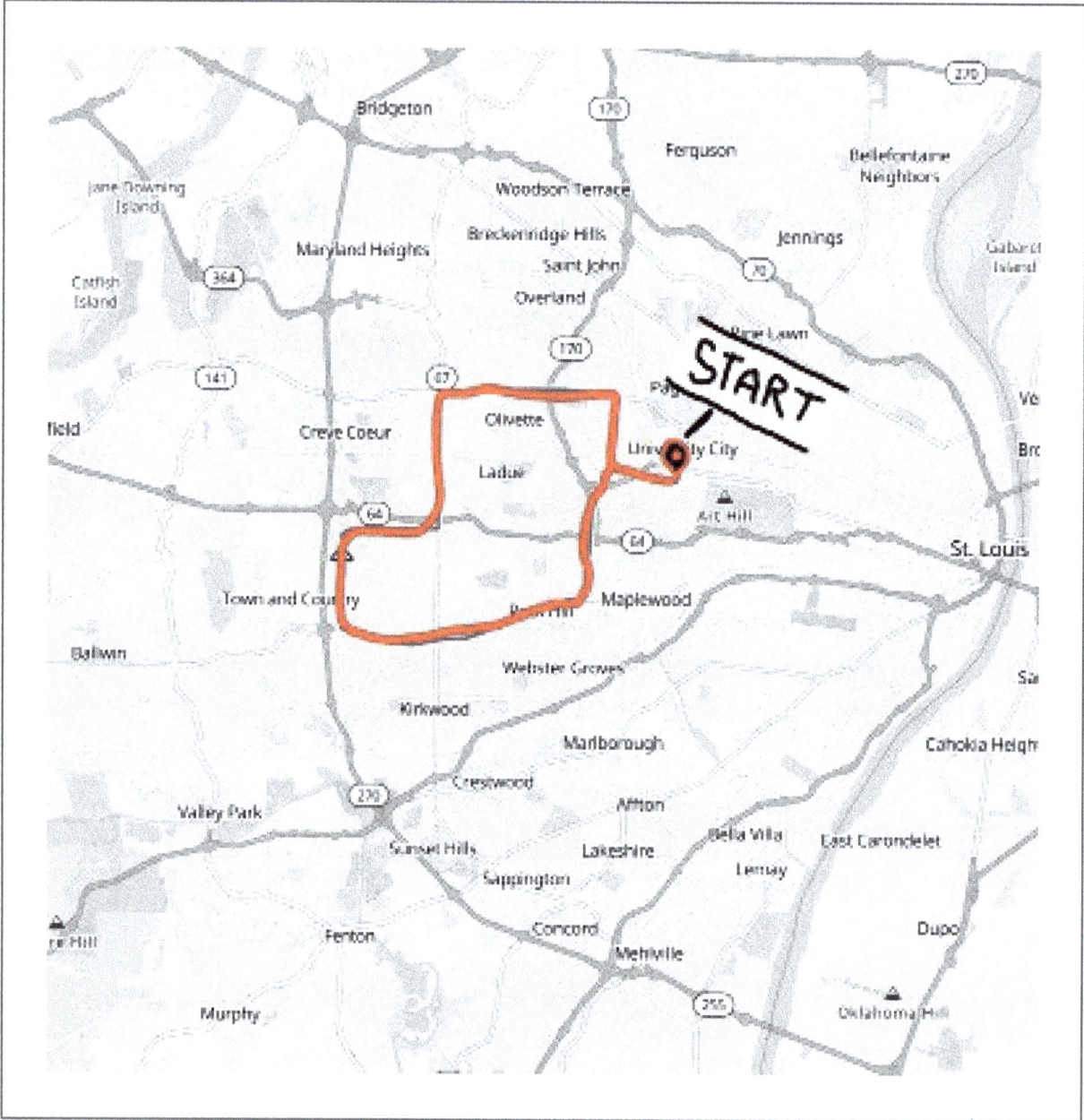

A map of the 1904 St. Louis marathon route.

CHAPTER 2

Starting with a blip about history...

A Chronicle of the Most Outrageous, Unconventional Olympic Marathon in History

BANG! It all started with a **BANG**! The pistol capped off just past three o'clock on this miserable, muggy, scorching hot Midwestern afternoon, and the announcement was made, "may the best man win."

(*Wendy, the school's historian, cleared her throat and continued overhead...*)

Runners representing four nations, the United States, South Africa, Cuba, and Greece were toe-to-toe at the starting line, already sweating bullets. Maybe from the pressure. Most likely from the stifling heat.

Two of the runners, men of the Tsuana tribe of South Africa, arrived at the starting line barefoot.

Thousands of sweltering spectators sat on the risers. Hand fans, hats, and sun umbrellas were a necessity; imagine a time when sunscreen was nonexistent.

9

This being the first time the United States hosted the Olympic Games made it monumental, and for many folks, the event was considered a first outing, altogether.

Hotdogs, soda, and games galore. The excitement was abundant, and so were the attractions and vendors.

What was not so abundant? Water.

You may ask, 'why not?' while pondering in depth about the genuine need that exists. For starters, water is a necessity for all.

In this case, it was summer, so the need increases. Now, consider the spectators.

Okay, never mind them. They had plenty of water.

More importantly, contemplate how lack of water affected the runners. This cruel and intentional experiment only included them.

A mistake? You thought.

Deliberate, unfortunately.

Yes. Intentional dehydration. Part of the plan. Really.

Think Guinea pigs. Lab rats. Victims of cruel and unusual circumstances if you will.

Seriously. Imagine an experiment that entails exposing humans to dangerous levels of heat and humidity while limiting water intake.

Yes, Olympic athletes.

Unbelievably, the runners were only able to secure water from two locations on the course. One, at the 6-mile marker and the other at the 12-mile marker because apparently, James Sullivan, the chief organizer of the games wanted to "minimize fluid intake to test the limits and effects of purposeful dehydration," a common area of research at the time.

I'm trying to hold back my sarcasm, but personally, I have to say, what a wonderful opportunity to do a bit of experimenting!

Seriously, I'm kidding!

Let me stay focused. I will continue the story.

The story about the Olympic Marathon, traditionally an honorary event established in ancient Greece, and historically, prestigious, but not in this case. Notably, looking back to this particular year of 1904, when we hosted the Games here in the United States as part of the World's Fair, it was quite a different experience. As you can imagine, the event resembled more a county fair, or more accurately, an exhibition regarded as a barbaric atrocity lacking humility—one that compromised the dignity of an Olympian.

Although the way things happened may sound implausible, or far-fetched, I can assure you in all disbelief, this is a true story!

I'm just getting started so listen up, friends!

(*Excitement propelled through Wendy's voice over the school's intercom system.*)

According to the local weather report, severe rainstorms swept through St. Louis days prior to the race, causing the 24.85-mile-long dirt course to wash away.

Yes. Dirt. It's 1904, think about it.

Reportedly, the alternate route that was mapped out by officials turned out to be even more challenging.

Sounds fair, right?

Totally normal. I'm afraid not.

More like, outrageous.

Consider the track. The terrain, composed of seven winding hills, was elevated as high as 300 ft and coated with a layer of thick dust, so it's clear to see, pun intended, how the runners were up against a trivial situation. One that posed significant health risks.

(*Wendy generally laughs aloud at her own puns, but this was no joking matter. She carried on.*)

I should also mention that throughout the race, the runners had to encounter people walking their dogs, and risk their lives cutting through cross-town traffic, while dodging delivery wagons, railroad trains, and trolley cars.

To make it worse, coaches and doctors, those put in place to help the runners, drove in cars, and rode horses alongside them, blowing dust directly into their lungs, sparking awful coughing attacks.

So, you may not be surprised to hear that William Garcia, an American competitor was discovered collapsed on the road along the marathon course with catastrophic respiratory injuries caused by inhaling dust.

I'm at a loss when trying to make sense as to how this all took place, especially considering the statistics! Let me tell you, the numbers are not good; out of the forty-one runners who signed up, only thirty-two actually started the race, and a total of fourteen, less than half finished.

I should say, survived!

...Yeah, that's more accurate. I'd like to report that there were fourteen Olympic marathon survivors.

You've heard about a couple of the South African contenders and the American, William Garcia from California. Now, let's look at the others.

I'll tell you all about their best and worst practices, and explain how the finalists managed to outrun or outsmart the others.

Starting with a runner from Cuba, a former mail carrier named, Félix Carbajal de Soto who had raised money to come to the states by demonstrating his running talent to his countrymen. He arrived at the starting line in despicable attire; wearing a ragged long-sleeved shirt, dark trousers, a pair of street shoes, and a beret, he was truly a sight to see. —Humiliating, to say the least. His pants were cut at the knee, by a fellow Olympian showing sympathy for his situation, exposing his long dark-colored dingy socks, and transforming his less-than-ideal racing uniform into an... Okay, ummm, let's say, a sportier, more aerodynamic, cooler version? Okay. I guess.

Picture his journey all the way from his home on the island. A boat. A plane. A long pit-stop in New Orleans where he lost all his money by gambling. Hitchhiking on foot to make it the rest of the way to St. Louis, he must have felt as though his luck ran out at the casino until a car stopped along the edge of the road. Finally. Just in time. He barely made it! What was he thinking? What compelled him to take such a chance? I mean, who does that? A true risk-taker! This explains his itch to gamble, perhaps.

Okay, back to the story...

There were a dozen Greek participants who had never run a marathon. They must have been disappointed. I mean, I feel bad that this was their first experience running a marathon, considering the subpar conditions, and not to mention, their first time in the United States.

How does this reflect upon our country? Our nation's standards?

I can't help but wonder.

The Americans, a group of experienced marathon runners included Sam Mellor, A.L. Newton, John Lordon, Michael Spring and Thomas Hicks; plus, I can't forget to mention Fredrick Lorz, a bricklayer by trade who worked to support his family during the day and trained for the marathon at night.

He earned his position on the Olympic team by placing in a five-mile race sponsored by the Amateur Athletic Union.

In fact, Fredrick Lorz was the first to cross the finish line! Yes, the amateur, who had dropped out after nine miles with the malintent to hitch a ride to the end; however, when his plan backfired and the car broke down at mile nineteen, he hopped back into the race and jogged his way to a fake victory.

Understandably, the crowd booed relentlessly, and officials disqualified him before the gold medal could be hung from his scrawny neck.

Serving him justice, the Amateur Athletic Union banned him for a year for his shenanigan. Notably, he carried on to eventually reclaiming his dignity by winning the 1905 Boston Marathon.

Looking at the second runner who managed to cross the line, Thomas Hicks. He ended up taking first place, thanks to his dishonest competitor. I must say, his success can be attributed to poison and egg whites. Crazy, I know! Picture this...

Around the 10-mile mark, he became ill. Showing signs of struggling, a support team stepped in to care for him throughout the remainder of the race. Failure was not an option!

Initially, he pled for a drink of water, however, they denied his request. No water! Part of the experiment. Alternately, they swabbed the inside of his mouth with warm distilled water. Then, seven miles from the finish line, they dosed him up with a potion consisting of strychnine; yes, the poison I mentioned, mixed with egg whites.

Reportedly, this is the first instance of performance enhancement drugs being used in the Olympic Games. You must know, Strychnine, in minimal doses, was often used as a stimulant, and during that time, it was not prohibited.

The poisonous concoction surged through Thomas' veins. He turned pale and began to stagger with limpness. Despite the slight setback, he heard the news that Fredrick Lorz had been disqualified and was able to gain a boost of energy. He began to jog slowly. To keep him going, his caretakers provided him with another dose of the toxic solution, along with a quick sponge bath, and unbelievably, his speed suddenly increased.

One race official reported, "Over the last two miles of the road, Hicks was running mechanically, like a well-oiled piece of machinery. His eyes were dull, lusterless; the ashen color of his face and skin had deepened; his arms appeared as weights well tied down; he could scarcely lift his legs, while his knees were almost stiff."

It was also reported that he was hallucinating at one point, and during his last mile, he begged for food and pleaded to lie down.

Did they let him, you ask? No!

At this point, you may wonder, how did he manage to stay alive, much less finish the marathon.

Okay, it was said that he was offered tea but refused. He gulped down two more egg whites while walking up an incline to tackle the last two hills and then jogged down as he shuffled into the stadium.

Now, this is the best part! For him to make it over the finish line, his trainers essentially lifted him slightly from the ground, while his feet moved back and forth.

He was proclaimed as the true, first-place winner!

As far as the other contenders, Len Tau, one of the South African participants, was chased a mile off course by feral dogs, and runner, John Lordon gave up after an extreme case of gagging, choking, and vomiting on the sidelines.

Honestly, I'm trying to picture this entire catastrophe and can't stop shaking my head in disbelief.

The outcome was disgraceful. Heinous. Almost barbaric. So much so that the event was nearly eliminated for good.

What a spectacle in St. Louis!

"...and that's all for today's historical, hysterical news," Wendy said, as she released the microphone button on the school's overhead PA system in the front office.

THE END

She got up from the secretary's chair after spinning twice and lowering it back to where it was when she sat down, realizing she had incredibly long legs. And skinny — probably why they've called her chicken legs since kindergarten.

Skipping down the hall towards her class with a smile on her face, she whistled a tune. It sounded like 'Three Blind Mice,' but no one could stop her long enough to find out.

... Beaming. Happy as a lark. She truly loves History. Not boring History. Fascinating, Funny History. The kind you begin reading and can't put down. Most of all, she finds reward in sharing her knowledge with her peers each morning.

Map of Poland.

CHAPTER 3

Starting with a blip about history...

Wojtek, 'Happy Warrior': The Polish Army's Recruited Brown Bear

Tick· Tick· Tick. It all started with a detonated catastrophic **BLAST!** Two blasts, as a matter of fact. Approximately, two weeks apart. One from each side.

(*Wendy, the school's historian, was wide-eyed and eager to tell her classmates more. She began over the loudspeaker...*)

Early on during World War II, Poland was invaded from two sides; both, Nazi Germany and Soviet Russia attempted to seize an opportunity to take control. Pun intended. Britain, having control over the Soviet army, forced them to release many Polish prisoners of war (POWs), and eventually, invalidated their land conquest in Poland.

The newly freed troops joined forces to become the Polish Free Army, military units that were divided and put to work where needed during the remainder of the war as directed by their country's allies. This army was formed under Władysław Anders, a Polish General also taken captive and then eventually released, and it is often referenced

19

as "Anders' Army." It makes sense, I guess.

(*Almost involuntarily, she found herself validating, or in some cases invalidating her findings; Wendy smirked semi-snidely, brushed her strawberry-blond hair back over her shoulder and chattered on telling this genuinely crazy story.*)

For many reasons, they are recognized as remarkable soldiers; however, it was their furriest recruit that made them world-renowned.

Basically, famous. Unforgettable. The most memorable, noteworthy, and presumably the only soldier that left a lasting impression is Wojtek, a Syrian brown bear.

Yes, a real bear. An orphaned cub. It's true.

Through his honor and dedication to service, he really made a name for himself!

For the record, his name, Wojtek means happy warrior, a nickname for the more common Polish name, Wojciech - pronounced VOY-tek.

He was a mercenary who found reward through serving a purpose.

Indeed, happy. Content. Cheerful. Carefree.

A well-deserving, courageous bear who was adopted by the troops, promoted within his battalion, and moved up the ranks as he gained more experience and exposure. — Exposure to things no other bear has encountered in all past accounts of history.

For good reason. Honestly. Bears should spend their days eating, relaxing, climbing trees, and foraging for food in preparation for the winter, hibernation season.

How was this even possible, you may ask, while your brain does a backflip and your eyes boggle in disbelief.

Trust me, I had to verify many sources to get all the facts, once I got a whiff of the story. Let me tell you more!

(*Wendy heard a bit of static in the overhead speakers, but she held the microphone steady and stayed focused. Going on...*)

When resources ran low, the Polish Free Army traveled out of the Soviet Union

wojtek

(VOY-tek)

through the Middle East, and into British leadership. Although, they lost countless soldiers to starvation, illness, and fatigue during the journey, they gained a new comrade, Wojtek.

A brave brown bear.

Still a cub, the soldiers bought him from a needy family at a train station near their temporary refugee camp in the Alborz Mountains of northern Iran. Having been separated from his mother at an early age, Wojtek had a lot to learn. He grew quickly and soon developed similar traits to his bunkmates; he greatly enjoyed cool showers, wrestling matches, swimming, and he found ways to pull his own weight around camp. Many of his newly acquired skills were practical and became useful during the war.

In fact, the 22nd Artillery Supply Company, a unit assigned to the Polish II Corps under British command, cared for him as one of their own.

Like family, they became inseparable.

Enjoying his company and seeing the calming effect he brought upon the troops, Lieutenant Anatol Tarnowieckikept made the decision to keep him. Sounds to me like Wojtek may be the very first service animal to have been adopted for his therapeutic qualities and ability to serve. Way before service animals were a thing. I feel this is a pun. Unintended, of course. Just comes naturally, I guess. Why am I so good at puns, without even trying?

(*Wendy steered herself out of another tangent just before she lost her train of thought. She was back on track and continued!*)

Yes, another pun. I'm sorry. Can't help it!

This bear was dynamic! Impressive! Remarkable! Extraordinary!

Astounding, at the very least.

Their newest recruit, 'Private Wojtek' was bottle-fed condensed milk, and soon developed a taste for coffee and cigarettes.

Wait. If you're wondering, how? Why? A bear, smoking? - No. Please don't fret too hard; he only swallowed the tobacco filled tubes. Doesn't sound safe. I know. It can't be much healthier, but certainly sounds like a more nutritious method of consumption. I mean, as opposed to inhaling carbon monoxide along with many other toxic chemicals, perhaps? —You think?

Debatable? No doubt. Dangerous? Definitely. Controversial? For sure.

Disgusting? Absolutely!

Working alongside his comrade soldiers, Wojtek's curated habits were undeniably humanistic. On the battle ground, he fiercely worked the front line. When it came to tasks, he demonstrated a ferocious desire and keen ability to carry artillery shells, crates weighing one hundred pounds each.

Oh yeah, and like any loyal recruit, he could stand straight and salute.

Still under the siege of Britain, their crew was forced to go to Italy to fight in the Battle of Monte Cassino, and according to strict regulations put in place by the port authority, animals were not allowed to board the ship.

The thought of separation was unbearable! (Yes, another pun.)

Finding themselves between a rock and a hard spot, they had to be savvy. Creative. Clever. They had to find a solution. A work-around. A way to keep Wojtek. And they did! They came up with a brilliant plan to draft him, rank him as a private, provide him with a serial number, and paybook.

Then, it became official; he was documented as an enlisted, active military soldier. A joyful brown bear. A satisfied serviceman. A happy warrior.

Still today, there are statues of him in Poland and Britain; seven to be exact.

I must also mention, he has memorials in the national war museums of Canada and Britain.

Wojtek. A legend. A hero.

Once the war came to an end, Wojtek retired from the military.

He was housed in Scotland at the Edinberg Zoo.

Admired, and well known, he had many visitors, you could imagine! Journalists, children, and often times, soldiers traveled to the zoo to visit the furry veteran.

The happy warrior was truly loved.

What a bear!

"...and that's all for today's historical, hysterical news," Wendy said, as she released the microphone button on the school's overhead PA system in the front office.

THE END

She turned to walk away just in time to see the secretary wiping a tear from her cheek as she approached the front desk.

Genuinely moved by the story, she told Wendy, "Thank you for sharing such interesting stories. The day would not be the same without you."

Wendy replied, "You're welcome, Ms. A!"

Gleaming bright as the sun, she skipped all the way down the hall to her first class, English, never breaking a smile. Not because she's super fond of English, but because she crazy about History!

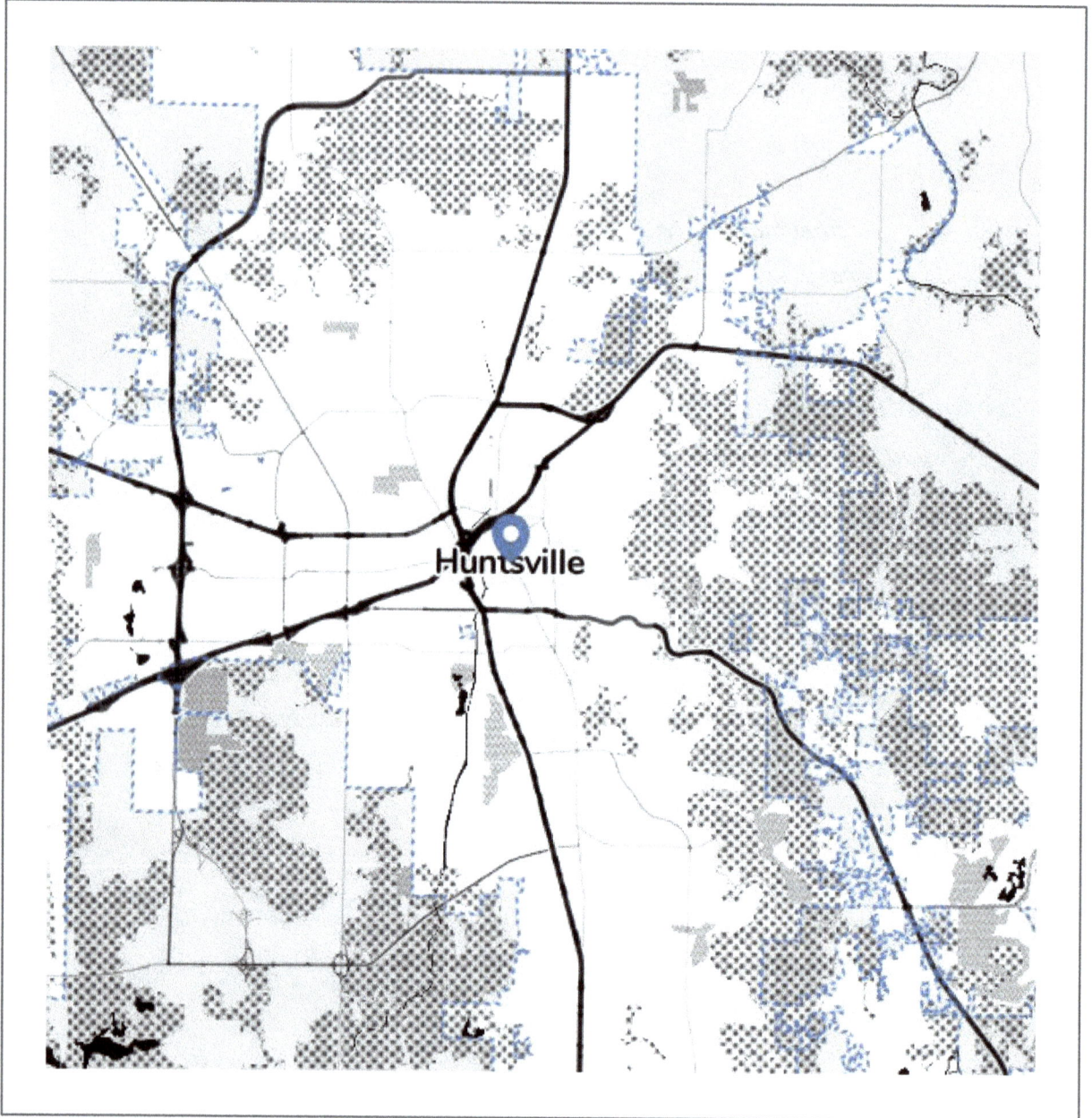

Huntsville, Alabama.

CHAPTER 4

THURSDAY: SCHOOL ANNOUNCEMENTS

Starting with a blip about history...

Space Exploration:
Experimenting With Fruit Flies

Buzzz. It all started with a faint **BUZZ**. Contained in a jar, strapped inside a rocket, and launched into the Final Frontier, fruit flies laid the foundation for human space travel.

(Wendy, the school's historian, spoke into the PA system's mic loud and clear...)

They also lay a lot of eggs. In general, I mean. A good thing, in this case. An attribute.

Specifically chosen because of their genetic structure, which is strikingly similar to humans, fruit flies have allotted NASA scientists an opportunity to conduct significant research.

You heard correctly, flying insects. Tiny pests. Prominent pioneers in astronautical engineering. Other fun facts: they are also the superstars that led researchers to a breakthrough in the study of genetics and biomedical science, plus they absolutely adore rotten bananas along with other decaying food. Anything containing yeast is their favorite!

What else makes them a spectacular specimen for experimentation and space exploration, you ask? They are teeny, lightweight, and can be maintained and cultured in small labs. Oh yeah, fruit flies grow quickly! It only takes them just around ten days to develop from an embryo into an adult, and they reproduce by the thousands.

I told you; they lay A LOT of eggs!

Were they the first species descended into space, you wonder? Ponder? Contemplate? Deliberate over the thought as your interest peaks and the intellectual side of you yearns to know more!?

(*Wendy, dying to get the details out, could not pass up an opportunity to go off on a short tangent. Redirecting herself, she gets back to the storyline...*)

Yes. Certainly they are not the only species propelled into the next dimension, but notably, fruit flies were indeed the first, and undeniably the most important specimen used in an extensive study involving the effects of cosmic radiation on organic matter, a subject our government knew little about at that time.

Shot into orbit in an unnamed V2 rocket from White Sands Missile Range in New Mexico, the flies traveled sixty-seven miles into the atmosphere before parachuting safely back to Earth. All part of a mission that took place on February 20, 1947, the first of many during Operation Paperclip.

Did your brain do a backbend upon learning of this news? A slight twirl? A cartwheel? Do you think I'm pulling your chain? Blowing hot air? Falsifying facts?

Distorting details to tell a good story?

I am not making this up. I promise. It was all part of a secret United States intelligence program.

So, you know, NASA pinpoints the elevation of sixty-six miles into the sky as the precise spot where space officially starts.

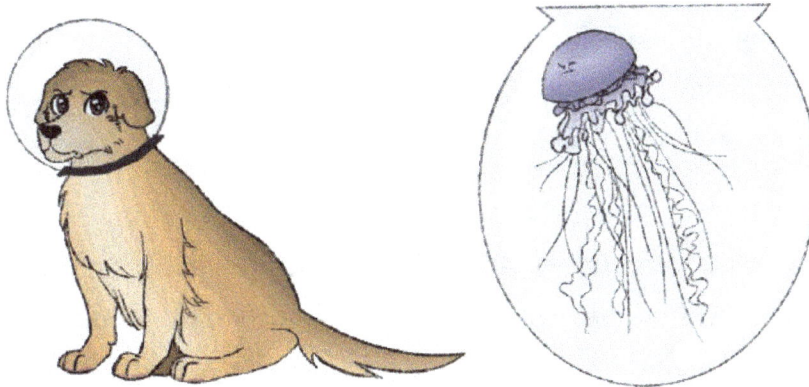

Many creatures have taken the trip. Monkeys. Mice. Dogs. Ants. Guinea Pigs. Spiders. Cockroaches. Cats. Fish. Frogs. Caterpillar moths. Worms. Wasps. Beetles.

Two Russian tortoises. Even jellyfish.

Sounds silly, but in this case, it's science.

Back to the fruit flies and their similarities to humans.

Strange. I know. Creepy. I agree.

Of course, you want to know more, even if a very tiny, microscopic part of your sensible side dismays the thought altogether, especially when considering the other, less favorable qualities for which these nasty little flying insects are famous. Specifically, if I were to mention the part about contamination and disease, you'd be totally grossed out. Disgusted. Repulsed. Sickened. Nauseated.

Hope you weren't eating breakfast. Please remember, I said famous, not glamorous, if that is what you're thinking.

Big difference in this case.

Sorry I brought it up, but it is true!

Most of all disease-causing genes found inside our bodies are also found in fruit flies. Not just their DNA, but also the way their cells work resembles our physiological structure. Their anatomy, also similar.

Can you believe, like humans, they have a gut, hair, brains, hearts, digestive tracts, reproductive organs, and muscles? Insane, right!? The way they function, need oxygen, food, and water to survive, and produce waste gives us an advantage in exploring space, as well as human growth and development.

Such useful little guys. And girls. Wait. I know we're not talking about worms which are classified as hermaphrodites, so this should not be debatable, but now that I'm telling the story, I'm wondering, can fruit flies be identified by gender? I may have to research that part more in-depth. It could be the topic of my next science essay, possibly.

(*Wendy took a mental note and continued. Still a faint buzz crackled in the loudspeakers. Yes, like the fruit flies in the jar, if you wondered, except louder, and more like a congested horse fly.*)

Okay, Operation Paperclip, shall I go on? I mean, it's a secret operation, so I don't know... ummm, if I am authorized to disclose more classified information. Okay, okay, settle down, I'm only kidding but, seriously, it is a project set into motion to exploit German science after the end of the Second World War. Although, it gave the United States government an opportunity to advance aeronautics, our military's primary focus was set towards gaining a technological advantage in the development of aircraft, rockets, and missiles at that time.

For good reason, since though German technology was deemed superior, and another war, the Cold War, was inevitably approaching as tensions grew stronger across the nation.

Many German scientists assisted our research efforts during the project including renowned Wernher von Braun, the scientist who designed the V2 missile.

Yes, the exact model the fruit flies comfortably took flight in. He also designed the Saturn V rocket for NASA, the same rocket that eventually landed humans on the moon in 1969.

Wernher von Braun's research group, employed by the division of the Army Ballistic Missile Agency, was assigned to work out of Redstone Arsenal in Huntsville, Alabama, the center of development for our country's ballistic missiles and nuclear weapons.

Keep in mind, V2s were the world's very first long-range guided missiles used by Germany during the Second World War. Imagine, a liquid propelled rocket that soars at a top speed of 3,500 miles per hour and demolishes targets over two hundred miles away! The United States military, dying to understand the ins and outs of how they were engineered, seized many of them to aid in research, after the war. A gruesome pun intended.

At one point, mammals became more involved in these types of studies; however, the fruit fly tests did not cease, and during 1952, the United States military established the Space Biology Laboratory at Holloman Air Force Base where laboratory director, Major David Simons spent a vast amount of time diligently moving flies, individually, one at a

time using tweezers, into capsules that were to be launched into orbit.

I bet you're thinking, what an assignment! Well, curiosity may or may not have killed the cat; no, not the one that they skyrocketed to space, but it certainly led me to daydream about what it would be like working in that lab, myself. —Fun? Maybe. Boring? Probably. Interesting? Only if you love science as much as that guy. Grueling, back-breaking labor? More than likely. —Perhaps his job was the type of job that causes an enormous amount of daily stress. Long hours. Reasonably, it would be hard to separate your work from your personal life, so forget the 'work-life balance' adults rave about. Think about it. You feel isolated. You begin to lose your hair. Naturally, your eyesight deteriorates from overuse. You develop frequent headaches, a loss of appetite, constipation, which in my mind, is better than dealing with diarrhea, while experiencing countless sleepless nights. —Then, when you finally fall asleep before reaching your breaking point, you have a horrific nightmare! Night sweats. Delirium.

Hypothetically, of course.

Seems as though, I'm not far off-base on this one, as it was noted that Major David Simons declared, "After you stare enough fruit flies straight in the eye, you start to hallucinate. I'm beginning to think I can see their eyelashes!"

What an experiment!

"...and that's all for today's historical, hysterical news," Wendy said, as she released the microphone button on the school's overhead PA system in the front office.

THE END

Her best friend, and president of the school's STEM club, sat next to her as she made the announcement this morning. They had planned to stop by the library on the way to class, but then remembered they had a vocabulary test in their English class, so they devised a new plan to go during lunch. Wendy needed a book to begin research on her next story.

A tall tale she could not wait to tell.

MAP: Boston, Massachusetts [North End]

CHAPTER 5

The Great Molasses Flood: Boston, 1919

RUMBLE! This odd disaster started with a **RUMBLE**, then a grumble. Next, a hiss followed by a very loud boom. A tsunami of dark, warm goop came about suddenly, demolishing anything and everything in its path, flooding the densely populated streets of Boston's North End, while engulfing citizens, bystanders, horses, and automobiles. This included nearby houses, buildings, and a two-story fire station. A deadly, and extremely sticky situation witnessed by many, most of whom became victims of the towering tidal wave of syrup. Truly a tragedy.

(*Wendy, the school's historian, pushed her glasses in place. Her slight smile morphed into a serious look, as she continued the grim tale.*)

Wondering how this happened on a whim? Concerned about the amount of syrup that flowed uncontrollably? Looking to learn how fast it traveled and who's responsible? Heavily contemplating the destruction this must've caused? Slightly curious how high the wave soared, while visualizing yourself surfing through the sweetness? — I do. Every time I tell this story.

Sounds like a lucid dream until you discover many people suffered severe injuries and then learn there were fatalities. Okay, admittedly more like a nightmare. The numbers aren't good; they're actually astounding.

This catastrophic calamity not only cost lives, but also more than one-hundred million dollars in damage.

Sadly, the sugary sludge also ended up in Boston Harbor, turning the water a disgusting shade of brown; and although I could, I will not go off on a tangent about the formation of bacteria that developed as a result.

Like most people aware of the atrocity, I have a tough time making sense of it all, but I've done a lot of research, so I will do my best to fill in the blanks.

Okay, where did it all go wrong, you want to know?

First off, many locals, residents of nearby neighborhoods, current and former employees, those most familiar with the Purity Distillery Company, a business that aided in the production of industrial alcohol, a substance used to make ammo during the First World War, were not shocked when the syrup tank burst, and then collapsed, so we cannot call it a 'whim'. — We are talking about a disaster that developed gradually, very slowly, like molasses. Because it was molasses.

The company stored a massive supply of the golden goop in the unsound reservoir.

Witnesses testified that over time, prior to the eruption, it often made gurgling noises and had ongoing leaks. Not a coincidence, they painted it brown, clearly, trying to conceal the amber-colored molasses percolating from the cracks, oozing from the inside out. So much so, it was said that visitors brought and filled their own containers from the architectural fractures.

Ummm, okay.

Sounds healthy.

Perfectly safe.

Totally normal, right?

Well...

Imagine Saturday morning. Your mom makes waffles. Excessively dry waffles. You realize, after searching the pantry, and under your sister's bed for ten minutes, there's no syrup. Why would she keep it under her bed, you ask? I don't have time to get into that now, as it could develop into a whole story of its own. A tangent. A long report no one has time to hear. One that could cause nausea. Nightmares. PTSD. Trust me. I will spare you.

So, back to the waffles. You're out of syrup. Your mom gives you an empty glass jar and sends you out. No money, just a jar. You realize it's an old grape jelly jar that has the stickers peeled off and although it's clean, the lid looks partially rusted.

Hoping your friends don't see you with that ugly thing, you head down the street on your bike, turn left, and there it is, the enormous brown vessel, drizzling over with molasses madness, just waiting to become part of your breakfast

In the aftermath of the tank's explosion, and during one of the most drawn-out lawsuits in history, attorneys, investigators, and other professionals scrambled to unravel the misfortunate circumstances. Endless hours were spent deliberating over the

details, as they clambered to sop up the facts for the court, the city's mayor, the victims, and the rest of the world. Although conclusions were made, the biggest question of how this could have been prevented remains.

According to the reports, had the Distillery taken precautionary measures during construction four years prior, they could have averted the whole molasses mishap, a freak accident that churned out a twenty five-foot wave of rich of raging syrup, 2.3 million gallons to be precise, at 35 miles per hour.

I know what you're thinking. Doesn't syrup seep slowly? Isn't the substance typically sluggish? Unreactive, altogether?

So true, but not under these unordinary circumstances. Several factors, including the unusually warm winter weather, played a part.

Now, let's examine the rickety, metal five-story structure itself. Constructed by the United States Industrial Alcohol Company four years prior, it stood ninety-feet high and fifty-feet wide. The court determined the Treasurer and Vice President of the company, Arthur P. Jell was put in charge of the project, and during trial, it became known that he cut corners to meet the final deadline. In a big rush to beat a steamer full of syrup coming from Cuba, the tank was erected in just three days and was never tested before filling; therefore, the fact it held syrup for several years leading up to the day of the casualty was no sign it was built compliant to the city's code, secure, stable, or safe.

Undoubtedly, the ongoing exterior leaks along with the internal gurgling noises heard bellowing from the belly of the beast had been of concern, not to mention the uneasy nature of molasses production, like a chemistry experiment, carbon dioxide produced by fermentation builds pressure. Another factor, a delivery of warm syrup was added to the existing cooler syrup, topping off the tank. Literally. Pun intended. Sorry.

This action offset a natural reaction that altered the viscosity of the two-million-gallon batch of brew. A deadly combination. Hitting the optimal capacity, the top torpedoed off. Metal rivets pushed to their limits, and unable to hold caused the side to split wide-open instantly, sounding off like a violent machine gun, witnesses testified.

Upon release, the turbulent torrent entrapped an entire district.

As it flowed through the streets, under the railway, and into the harbor, the consistency of the substance changed. Settling waist high, increasingly difficult to manage, it thickened and hardened around people and objects like peanut brittle candy.

Rescue efforts included the Boston Police Department, local firefighters, medical staff from Haymarket Square Relief Station, plus over one hundred sailors from Nantucket. At first, they tried drills and chisels. Power tools were no match for the mess.

Next, they used brine, a solution of saltwater to power-wash the solid cemented sugar off the glazed city surfaces. Proving effective, rescue workers were able to free those stuck in the muck.

As I report the details, I think of the syrup left behind on my breakfast plate after eating pancakes. Part of my weekend chores include tackling dishes, so I've learned that it becomes stubborn like glue, and does not easily come off once it hardens! May be the reason I'm told to rinse my dishes after I eat. Makes sense, I will admit. Not to my parents.

Of course.

Imagine the residents. Like the hardened residue left behind, confusion, sheer panic, and paranoia set in across the city. Relying on different news sources and the local media to deliver an accurate account of the facts, Bostonians were truly at a loss.

What a shamble! A very sticky one.

"...and that's all for today's historical, hysterical news," Wendy said, as she released the microphone button on the school's overhead PA system in the front office.

THE END

Feeling relieved to have made it through the story without stuttering, she laughed quietly at herself. Her priority at this point was breakfast. Perhaps all the talk about pancakes made her extra hungry. Arriving at the cafeteria, she discovered zero pancakes. Just a muffin. Apple cinnamon. Prepackaged. Not the best.

"Better than nothing," she said to herself as she crammed at least half in her mouth on her way down the hall while forgetting her carton of milk. With no time to turn back, she keeps going. Smart choice. The bell rang.

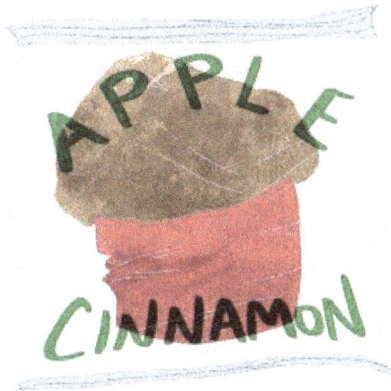

aerodynamic – a branch of dynamics that deals with the motion of air and other gaseous fluids and with the forces acting on bodies in motion relative to such fluids.

aeronautics – a science dealing with the operation of aircraft.

allotted – assigned or distributed as a portion, share, or lot.

ashen – resembling ashes (as in color).

atrocity – a shockingly bad or atrocious act, object, or situation.

attire – dress clothes.

attribute – a word ascribing a quality.

battalion – a considerable body of troops organized to act together.

beret – visorless usually woolen cap with a tight headband and a soft full flat top.

biomedicine – medicine based on the application of the principles of the natural sciences and especially biology and biochemistry.

carbon dioxide – a heavy colorless gas CO_2 that does not support combustion, dissolves in water to form carbonic acid, is formed especially in animal respiration and in the decay or combustion of animal and vegetable matter, is absorbed from the air by plants in photosynthesis, and is used in the carbonation of beverages.

carbon monoxide – a colorless odorless very toxic gas CO that is formed as a product of the incomplete combustion of carbon or a carbon compound.

casino – a building or room used for social amusements; specifically: one used for gambling.

compelled – to drive or urge forcefully or irresistibly.

comrade – an intimate friend or associate.

concoction – something (such as a food or drink) that is concocted from various elements.

condensed milk – evaporated milk with sugar added.

controversy – a discussion marked especially by the expression of opposing views.

curated – carefully chosen and thoughtfully organized or presented.

detonated – to explode with sudden violence.

distilled water – water that has been freed of dissolved or suspended solids and from organisms by distillation (as for medical or chemical purposes).

embryo – a vertebrate at any stage of development prior to birth or hatching.

exploit – to make use of meanly or unfairly for one's own advantage.

GLOSSARY

fatalities – the quality or state of causing death or destruction.

fermentation – the enzyme-catalyzed anaerobic breakdown of an energy-rich compound (such as a carbohydrate to carbon dioxide and alcohol or to an organic acid) by the action of microorganisms (such as bacteria or yeast) that occurs naturally.

Genetic – relating to or determined by the origin, development, or causal antecedents of something.

hallucinate – to affect with visions or imaginary perceptions.

heinous – hatefully or shockingly evil.

hermaphrodite – an animal or plant having both male and female reproductive organs, structures, or tissue.

hypothetically – by making an assumption for the sake of discussion or argument.

implausible – not plausible: provoking disbelief.

law of gravity – the gravitational attraction of the mass of the earth, the moon, or a planet for bodies at or near its surface.

physiological – characteristic of or appropriate to an organism's healthy or normal functioning.

prominent – readily noticeable.

pun – the usually humorous use of a word in such a way as to suggest two or more of its meanings or the meaning of another word similar in sound.

pungent – having an intense flavor or odor.

refugee – a person who flees to a foreign country or power to escape danger or persecution.

reservoir - a place where something is kept in store.

savvy - practical know-how.

scarcely – by a narrow margin.

shad – any of several fishes (especially genus Alosa) of the herring family that differ from the typical herrings (genus Clupeus) in having a relatively deep body and in being anadromous and that include some important food fishes of Europe and North America.

shenanigan – a devious trick used especially for an underhand purpose.

stimulant – an agent (such as a drug) that produces a temporary increase of the functional activity or efficiency of an organism or any of its parts.

GLOSSARY

strychnine – a bitter poisonous alkaloid $C_{21}H_{22}N_2O_2$ that is obtained from nux vomica and related plants (genus Strychnos) and is used as a poison (as for rodents) and medicinally as a stimulant of the central nervous system.

subpar – below a usual or normal level or standard.

sustain – to give support or relief to.

tangent – diverging from an original purpose or course.

torrent - a violent or forceful flow of fluid.

trolley - a streetcar powered electrically.

trousers – pants.

tsunami – a great sea wave produced especially by submarine earth movement or volcanic eruption.

world-renowned – known and admired throughout the world: world-famous.

BIBLIOGRAPHY

Abbott, Karen. "The 1904 Olympic Marathon May Have Been the Strangest Ever." Smithsonian Magazine. 7 Aug. 2012.

Collins, Dac. "Winter Storm Makes It Rain Fish in Texarkana; Residents Scoop Up Free Bait." Outdoor Life. 3 Jan. 2022.

Collins, Turner. "Wojtek: The Bear Who Fought for Poland in World War II." The Collector. 19 July 2022.

Dunn, Lori. "Storm Rains Bushels of Fish on Texarkana." Texarkana Gazette. 29 Dec. 2021.

Education Northwest. (2011). Spotlight on the common core state standards. Retrieved from Education Northwest

Geib, Samantha, "Research Strategies Award Essay: The Boston Molasses Disaster." Ames Library Awards, Digital Commons. Illinois Wesleyan University. Apr. 2010.

Gilbert, Asha C. "Fish Rain from the Sky during Storm in Eastern Texas." USA TODAY. 31 Dec. 2021.

Hanson, Molly. "The Most Bizarre Marathon in Olympic History." Run, Powered by Outside. Outside. 29 July 2021.

"How are Insects and Human Similar?" Beetle Dissection. Ask A Biologist. Arizona State University.

Jabr, Ferris. "The Science of the Great Molasses Flood." Scientific American. vol. 309, no. 2, Scientific American, a Division of Nature America, Inc., doi:10.2307/26017904. 1 Aug. 2013.

BIBLIOGRAPHY

J Joose. Tess. "February 1947: The First Animals, Fruit Flies, Rocket into Space and Return to Earth." APS News, vol. 32, no. 2. This Month in Physics History. American Physical Society. 12 Jan. 2023.

Kennon, Joshua. "Lessons from the Great Boston Molasses Flood of 1919." Joshua Kennon, Thoughts on Business, Politics, and Life. 12 Jun. 2015.

Killian, Aaron. "The Great Molasses Flood of 1919." Historic America. 19 Jan. 2015.

Lusher, Adam. "Wojtek: The Bear Who Fought Hitler's Nazis." The Independent. 24 Sept. 2018.

McCarthy, Meghan. "The Wildest Race Ever: The Story of the 1904 Olympic Marathon." Simon and Schuster. Mar 1, 2016.

McCullar, Emily. "Fish Fell from the Sky in Texarkana, and No One Is Reel-y Sure Why." Texas Monthly. 4 Jan. 2022.

Merriam-Webster. An Encyclopedia Britannica Company.

Neufeld, Michael. "Project Paperclip and American Rocketry after World War II." National Air and Space Museum. Smithsonian. 31 Mar. 2023.

Tousignant, Marylou. "In World War II, a Bear Became Companion and Helper to Polish Soldiers," The Washington Post, 30 Aug. 2021.

"V-2 Missile." National Air and Space Museum. Smithsonian. 3 Aug. 2000.

Wasser, Miriam. "What Did 2.3 Million Gallons of Molasses Do to Boston Harbor? WBUR News. 15 Jan. 2019.

BIBLIOGRAPHY

"What Was the First Animal in Space?" Royal Museums Greenwich.

PEOPLE

PLACES AND EVENTS

PLACES AND EVENTS

PLACES AND EVENTS

A literacy advocate and emerging indie author, **Wendy** takes a humorous, narrative approach to **creative nonfiction** — a genre traditionally considered dry. Aimed to educate and entertain middle school-aged readers, her first book of a series, **Historical, Hysterical Tangents – Book 1** features a collection of short stories based on **unimaginable** events that actually happened. They are full of facts, no doubt. Overrunning with fun, indeed. **Knee deep in puns**? Of course!

Wendy's broad collegiate studies in liberal arts include ethics, psychology, literature, public relations, communications, mass media, history, theatre, plus creative and technical writing. — Focused on helping young scholars pursue their dreams, she leverages her talent to inspire at the community level. Building a career in public **education**, she positions herself to mentor a diverse, underrepresented group of students in college and career readiness, as well as a broad range of core subjects essential for high school graduation.

Now, affirming her commitment to creating opportunities for herself and others, she extends her passion for literature, research, cultural writing, and storytelling through **independent self-publishing**.

Growing up in Michigan, The Great Lakes State, she attended summer camp each year where she developed a **love** for the outdoors, swimming, racquetball, photography, reading, and journaling. Oh yeah, and apples. — Michigan has a lot of apples. As an only child with no siblings, Wendy spent most of her time forging connections with her peers.

She quickly discovered that mentoring others offers her a sense of **purpose**. – it's her **passion**.

ABOUT THE ILLUSTRATOR

As an up-and-coming illustrator who's been drawn to storytelling since childhood, **Jack's** focus evolves around animation. More recently, he spends his time working on illustrating books for print. By flipping through the pages in this neatly crafted book, you can see for yourself, he's pretty darn **amazing**!

Continually sharpening his pencils and drawing skills through self-development, Jack **dreams** of creating cartoons that are both fun and meaningful for audiences of all ages. Taking special interests in character and background creation, his work brings entire worlds to **life**—one sketch at a time.

Jack loves animals, roller skating, and cranking up loud heavy music—basically, he lives life on the wild side! He also dotes on his two aquarium clownfish, **Swim Shady** and **Taylor Swish**—because even his pets have a killer stage presence.